A
LITTLE
TREASURY OF
Love Poems
❖❖❖

✿✿✿✿✿✿✿✿✿✿✿✿✿✿✿✿✿✿✿✿✿✿✿✿✿

A
LITTLE
TREASURY OF
Love Poems

EDITED BY
CARY WILKINS

✿✿✿

Many waters cannot quench love,
neither can the floods drown it.
The Song of Solomon

✿✿✿

AVENEL BOOKS
New York

✿✿✿✿✿✿✿✿✿✿✿✿✿✿✿✿✿✿✿✿✿✿✿✿✿

Copyright © 1980 by Crown Publishers, Inc.
All rights reserved
This 1982 edition is published by Avenel Books,
distributed by Crown Publishers, Inc.
Manufactured in the United States of America
Library of Congress Cataloging in Publication Data
Main entry under title
ISBN: 0-517 375621

h g f e d

Contents

❂❂❂❂

Introduction

From the Bible to Shakespeare to Whitman and Dickinson, the face of love in poetry through the ages has changed. But the soul of love, which a good poem ultimately reveals, has remained the same. The joys and sorrows, ecstasies and agonies of love are universal qualities that will never change.

Love between friends, love between a dog and his master, love for one's neighbor or oneself—most of the poems in this book do not extol these kinds of love. Instead, they describe the fireworks caused by the first meeting of two pairs of eyes, the longing of one soul for another, the longing of one anatomical part for another, "two hearts beating each to each"— in short, Love with a capital L.

A great many love poems have become popular favorites, and many of these are included in this collection, along with a few interesting, unfamiliar ones.

The poems are roughly grouped according to attitudes toward and stages of love. Opening the collection, we have Shakespeare, Ben Jonson, Andrew Marvell, and others reminding us that the time for love is now, today: "Time will not be ours for ever,/ He at length, our good will sever."

Next we have many interesting definitions of love from Sir Walter Ralegh, Samuel Daniel, Blake, Robert Browning, Shelley, and Keats. Everyone has his own definition of love, and you will find almost all of them here: "that fountain and that well," "a sunshine mix'd with rain," "a thing that creeps," "a sickness full of woes," "Summer redundant,/Blueness abundant," "a doll dress'd up."

Following these are several poems in which a lovesick wooer entreats some cruel person to end his or her heartache. Some are not so desperate, as in Christopher Marlowe's inviting poem "The Passionate Shepherd to His Love."

Once the lovers have been united, we have many poets singing the joys of love and singing the praises of their loved ones: Tennyson, Dante Gabriel Rossetti, Elizabeth Barrett Browning, Byron, Whitman, Wordsworth, and many others. In contrast to Edgar Allan Poe's lofty tribute "To Helen" is Andrew Lang's poem "To Helen," a terrific bowler.

Some loves are like evergreens, but some bloom and fade with the seasons. Farewells are difficult, but they can at least be done with style, as expressed here by Byron, Shelley, and others. For those who can survive the rough times, the rewards are sometimes great. Emerson, Wordsworth, Anne Bradstreet, and Robert Browning are among those who think so.

With the last few poems in the book, we sail away from earth into the shadowy realm of dreams and the poignant, empty world of separated lovers. Christina Rossetti, John Donne, and Matthew Arnold are among those who offer glimpses into the sometimes painful, sometimes comforting dreams of lovers.

Most everyone will agree that love will always make the world go round. From biblical times to the early 1900s, the poems here show that Love with a capital L has not changed over the centuries.

CARY WILKINS

O MISTRESS MINE

from *Twelfth Night*

❖❖❖

O mistress mine, where are you roaming?
O, stay and hear! your true-love's coming
    That can sing both high and low;
Trip no further, pretty sweeting,
Journeys end in lovers' meeting,—
    Every wise man's son doth know.

What is love? 't is not hereafter;
Present mirth hath present laughter;
    What's to come is still unsure:
In delay there lies no plenty,—
Then come kiss me, Sweet-and-twenty,
    Youth 's a stuff will not endure.

William Shakespeare

SONG: TO CELIA

Come, my Celia, let us prove,
While we may, the sports of love;
Time will not be ours for ever,
He, at length, our good will sever.
Spend not then his gifts in vain.
Suns, that set, may rise again:
But, if once we loose this light,
'T is, with us, perpetual night.
Why should we defer our joys?
Fame, and rumour are but toys.
Cannot we delude the eyes
Of a few poor household spies?
Or his easier ears beguile,
So removed by our wile?
'T is no sin, love's fruit to steal,
But the sweet theft to reveal:
To be taken, to be seen,
These have crimes accounted been.

Ben Jonson

TO HIS COY MISTRESS

Had we but world enough, and time,
This coyness, lady, were no crime.
We would sit down, and think which way
To walk, and pass our long love's day.

Thou by the Indian Ganges' side
Should'st rubies find: I by the tide
Of Humber would complain. I would
Love you ten years before the flood,
And you should, if you please, refuse
Till the conversion of the Jews;
My vegetable love should grow
Vaster than empires and more slow;
An hundred years should go to praise
Thine eyes, and on thy forehead gaze;
Two hundred to adore each breast,
But thirty thousand to the rest;
An age at least to every part,
And the last age should show your heart.
For, lady, you deserve this state,
Nor would I love at lower rate.

But at my back I always hear
Time's winged chariot hurrying near,
And yonder all before us lie
Deserts of vast eternity.
Thy beauty shall no more be found,
Nor, in thy marble vault, shall sound
My echoing song: then worms shall try
That long preserved virginity,
And your quaint honour turn to dust,
And into ashes all my lust:
The grave's a fine and private place,
But none, I think, do there embrace.

Now therefore, while the youthful hue
Sits on thy skin like morning dew,
And while thy willing soul transpires
At every pore with instant fires,

Now let us sport us while we may,
And now, like amorous birds of prey
Rather at once our time devour,
Than languish in his slow-chaped power.
Let us roll all our strength and all
Our sweetness up into one ball,
And tear our pleasures with rough strife,
Thorough the iron gates of life;
Thus, though we cannot make our sun
Stand still, yet we will make him run.

Andrew Marvell

TO THE VIRGINS
TO MAKE MUCH OF TIME

❂❀❂❀❂

Gather ye rose-buds while ye may,
  Old Time is still a-flying:
And this same flower that smiles today,
  Tomorrow will be dying.

The glorious lamp of heaven, the Sun,
  The higher he's a-getting
The sooner will his race be run,
  And nearer he's to setting.

That age is best which is the first,
  When youth and blood are warmer;
But being spent, the worse, and worst
  Times, still succeed the former.

Then be not coy, but use your time;
    And while ye may, go marry:
For having lost but once your prime,
    You may for ever tarry.

Robert Herrick

MY SWEETEST LESBIA

My sweetest Lesbia, let us live and love;
And though the sager sort our deeds reprove,
Let us not weigh them: heaven's great lamps do dive
Into their west, and straight again revive:
But soon as once set is our little light,
Then must we sleep one ever-during night.

If all would lead their lives in love like me,
Then bloody swords and armour should not be;
No drum nor trumpet peaceful sleeps should move,
Unless alarm came from the camp of love:
But fools do live, and waste their little light,
And seek with pain their ever-during night.

When timely death my life and fortune ends,
Let not my hearse be vext with mourning friends;
But let all lovers, rich in triumph, come
And with sweet pastimes grace my happy tomb:
And, Lesbia, close up thou my little light,
And crown with love my ever-during night.

Thomas Campion

THE SHEPHERD'S
DESCRIPTION OF LOVE

Shepherd, what's love? I pray thee tell.
It is that fountain, and that well,
Where pleasure and repentance dwell:
It is, perhaps, that saucing bell,
    That tolls all into heaven or hell:
    And this is love, as I heard tell.

Yet what is love? I prithee say.
It is a work on holyday,
It is December match'd with May,
When lusty bloods in fresh array
    Hear ten months after of the play:
    And this is love, as I hear say.

Yet what is love? good Shepherd sain.
It is a sunshine mix'd with rain;
It is a toothach; or like pain;
It is a game, where none doth gain.
    The lass saith no, and would full fain:
    And this is love, as I hear sain.

Yet, Shepherd, what is love, I pray?
It is a yea, it is a nay,
A pretty kind of sporting fray,
It is a thing will soon away;
    Then nymphs take 'vantage while ye may:
    And this is love, as I hear say.

Yet what is love? good Shepherd show.
A thing that creeps, it cannot go;
A prize that passeth to and fro,
A thing for one, a thing for mo,
    And he that proves shall find it so,
    And, Shepherd, this is love I trow.

Sir Walter Ralegh

["THEY SIN WHO TELL US LOVE CAN DIE"]

from *The Curse of Kehama*

They sin who tell us Love can die.
    With life all other passions fly,
        All others are but vanity.
    In Heaven Ambition cannot dwell,
    Nor Avarice in the vaults of Hell;
    Earthly these passions of the Earth,
They perish where they have their birth;
        But Love is indestructible.
    Its holy flame for ever burneth,
From Heaven it came, to Heaven returneth;
    Too oft on Earth a troubled guest,
    At times deceived, at times opprest,
        It here is tried and purified,
    Then hath in Heaven its perfect rest:
    It soweth here with toil and care,
But the harvest time of Love is there.

Robert Southey

LOVE IS A SICKNESS

✿✚✿✚✿

Love is a sickness full of woes,
    All remedies refusing;
A plant that most with cutting grows,
    Most barren with best using.
        Why so?
More we enjoy it, more it dies;
If not enjoyed, it sighing cries
        Heigh-ho!

Love is a torment of the mind,
    A tempest everlasting;
And Jove hath made it of a kind,
    Not well, nor full, nor fasting.
        Why so?
More we enjoy it, more it dies;
If not enjoyed, it sighing cries
        Heigh-ho!

Samuel Daniel

TELL ME, MY HEART, IF THIS BE LOVE

✿✚✿✚✿

When Delia on the plain appears,
Awed by a thousand tender fears,
I would approach, but dare not move;—
Tell me, my heart, if this be love.

Whene'er she speaks, my ravished ear
No other voice than hers can hear;
No other wit but hers approve;—
Tell me, my heart, if this be love.

If she some other swain commend,
Though I was once his fondest friend,
His instant enemy I prove;—
Tell me, my heart, if this be love.

When she is absent, I no more
Delight in all that pleased before,
The clearest spring, the shadiest grove;—
Tell me, my heart, if this be love.

When fond of power, of beauty vain,
Her nets she spread for every swain,
I strove to hate, but vainly strove;—
Tell me, my heart, if this be love.

George Lord Lyttelton

THE CLOD AND THE
PEBBLE

❂❂❂

"Love seeketh not Itself to please,
Nor for itself hath any care,
But for another gives its ease,
And builds a Heaven in Hell's despair."

So sung a little Clod of Clay
Trodden with the cattle's feet.
But a Pebble of the brook
Warbled out these metres meet:

"Love seeketh only Self to please,
To bind another to Its delight,
Joys in another's loss of ease,
And builds a Hell in Heaven's despite."

William Blake

T O ——

Music, when soft voices die,
Vibrates in the memory—
Odours, when sweet violets sicken,
Live within the sense they quicken.

Rose leaves, when the rose is dead,
Are heaped for the beloved's bed;
And so thy thoughts, when thou art gone,
Love itself shall slumber on.

Percy Bysshe Shelley

WANTING IS — WHAT?

from *Jocoseria*

❁❁❁❁

Wanting is—what?
Summer redundant,
Blueness abundant,
—Where is the blot?
Beamy the world, yet a blank all the same,
—Framework which waits for a picture to frame:
What of the leafage, what of the flower?
Roses embowering with nought they embower!
Come then, complete incompletion, O comer,
Pant through the blueness, perfect the summer!
Breathe but one breath
Rose-beauty above,
And all that was death
Grows life, grows love,
Grows love!

Robert Browning

AH, HOW SWEET

❁❁❁❁

Ah, how sweet it is to love!
Ah, how gay is young desire!
And what pleasing pains we prove
When we first approach love's fire!
Pains of love are sweeter far
Than all other pleasures are.

Sighs which are from lovers blown
  Do but gently heave the heart:
E'en the tears they shed alone
  Cure, like trickling balm, their smart.
Lovers, when they lose their breath,
Bleed away in easy death.

Love and Time with reverence use,
  Treat them like a parting friend;
Nor the golden gifts refuse
  Which in youth sincere they send:
For each year their price is more,
And they less simple than before.

Love, like spring-tides full and high,
  Swells in every youthful vein;
But each tide does less supply,
  Till they quite shrink in again.
If a flow in age appear,
'T is but rain, and runs not clear.

John Dryden

GIVE ALL TO LOVE
❁❀❁❀

Give all to love;
Obey thy heart;
Friends, kindred, days,
Estate, good-fame,
Plans, credit and the Muse,—
Nothing refuse.

'T is a brave master;
Let it have scope:
Follow it utterly,
Hope beyond hope:
High and more high
It divides into noon,
With wing unspent,
Untold intent;
But it is a god,
Knows its own path
And the outlets of the sky.

It was never for the mean;
It requireth courage stout.
Souls above doubt,
Valor unbending,
It will reward,—
They shall return
More than they were,
And ever ascending.

Leave all for love;
Yet, hear me, yet,
One word more thy heart behoved,
One pulse more of firm endeavor,—
Keep thee to-day,
To-morrow, forever,
Free as an Arab
Of thy beloved.

Cling with life to the maid;
But when the surprise,
First vague shadow of surmise
Flits across her bosom young,
Of a joy apart from thee,

Free be she, fancy-free;
Nor thou detain her vesture's hem,
Nor the palest rose she flung
From her summer diadem.

Though thou loved her as thyself,
As a self of purer clay,
Though her parting dims the day,
Stealing grace from all alive;
Heartily know,
When half-gods go,
The gods arrive.

Ralph Waldo Emerson

MODERN LOVE

❂❂❂

And what is love? It is a doll dress'd up
For idleness to cosset, nurse, and dandle;
A thing of soft misnomers, so divine
That silly youth doth think to make itself
Divine by loving, and so goes on
Yawning and doting a whole summer long,
Till Miss's comb is made a pearl tiara,
And common Wellingtons turn Romeo boots;
Then Cleopatra lives at number seven,
And Antony resides in Brunswick Square.
Fools! if some passions high have warm'd the world,
If Queens and Soldiers have play'd deep for hearts,

It is no reason why such agonies
Should be more common than the growth of weeds.
Fools! make me whole again that weighty pearl
The Queen of Egypt melted, and I'll say
That ye may love in spite of beaver hats.

John Keats

PRIDE OF YOUTH

Even as a child, of sorrow that we give
    The dead, but little in his heart can find,
    Since without need of thought to his clear mind
Their turn it is to die and his to live:—
Even so the winged New Love smiles to receive
    Along his eddying plumes the auroral wind,
    Nor, forward glorying, casts one look behind
Where night-rack shrouds the Old Love fugitive.

There is a change in every hour's recall,
    And the last cowslip in the fields we see
    On the same day with the first corn-poppy.
Alas for hourly change! Alas for all
The loves that from his hand proud Youth lets fall,
    Even as the beads of a told rosary!

Dante Gabriel Rossetti

from *EPIPSYCHIDION*

True Love in this differs from gold and clay,
That to divide is not to take away.
Love is like understanding, that grows bright,
Gazing on many truths; 'tis like thy light,
Imagination! which from earth and sky,
And from the depths of human phantasy,
As from a thousand prisms and mirrors, fills
The Universe with glorious beams, and kills
Error, the worm, with many a sun-like arrow
Of its reverberated lightning. Narrow
The heart that loves, the brain that contemplates,
The life that wears, the spirit that creates
One object, and one form, and builds thereby
A sepulchre for its eternity.

Mind from its object differs most in this:
Evil from good; misery from happiness;
The baser from the nobler; the impure
And frail, from what is clear and must endure.
If you divide suffering and dross, you may
Diminish till it is consumed away;
If you divide pleasure and love and thought,
Each part exceeds the whole; and we know not
How much, while any yet remains unshared,
Of pleasure may be gained, of sorrow spared:
The truth is that deep well, whence sages draw
The unenvied light of hope; the eternal law
By which those live, to whom this world of life
Is as a garden ravaged, and whose strife
Tills for the promise of a later birth
The wilderness of this Elysian earth.

Percy Bysshe Shelley

26

SONNET CXVI

Let me not to the marriage of true minds
Admit impediments. Love is not love
Which alters when it alteration finds,
Or bends with the remover to remove.
O no! it is an ever-fixed mark
That looks on tempests, and is never shaken;
It is the star to every wandering bark,
Whose worth's unknown, although his height be
    taken.
Love's not Time's fool, though rosy lips and cheeks
Within his bending sickle's compass come;
Love alters not with his brief hours and weeks,
But bears it out even to the edge of doom.
    If this be error and upon me proved,
    I never writ, nor no man ever loved.

William Shakespeare

["ALTER? WHEN THE HILLS DO"]

Alter? When the hills do.
Falter? When the sun
Question if his glory
Be the perfect one.

Surfeit? When the daffodil
Doth of the dew:
Even as herself, O friend!
I will of you!

Emily Dickinson

THE PASSIONATE
SHEPHERD
TO HIS LOVE

Come live with me and be my love,
And we will all the pleasures prove
That hills and valleys, dales and fields,
Or woods and steepy mountains yields.

And we will sit upon the rocks
Seeing the shepherds feed their flocks,
By shallow rivers, to whose falls
Melodious birds sing madrigals.

And I will make thee beds of roses
And a thousand fragrant posies,
A cap of flowers, and a kirtle
Embroidered all with leaves of myrtle;

A gown made of the finest wool,
Which from our pretty lambs we pull;
Fair linèd slippers for the cold,
With buckles of the purest gold;

A belt of straw and ivy buds
With coral clasps and amber studs:
And if these pleasures may thee move,
Come live with me and be my love.

The shepherd swains shall dance and sing
For thy delight each May morning:
If these delights thy mind may move,
Then live with me and be my love.

Christopher Marlowe

THE NYMPH'S REPLY

❁❁❁❁❁

If that the world and love were young,
And truth in every shepherd's tongue,
These pretty pleasures might me move
To live with thee and be thy love.

But time drives flocks from field to fold,
When rivers rage, and rocks grow cold;
And Philomel becometh dumb,
And all complain of cares to come.

The flowers do fade, and wanton fields
To wayward winter reckoning yields;
A honey tongue, a heart of gall,
Is fancy's spring, but sorrow's fall.

Thy gowns, thy shoes, thy beds of roses,
Thy cap, thy kirtle, and thy posies
Soon break, soon wither, soon forgotten,—
In folly ripe, in reason rotten.

Thy belt of straw and ivy buds,
Thy coral clasps and amber studs,—
All these in me no means can move
To come to thee, and be thy love.

But could youth last, and love still breed,
Had joys no date, nor age no need,
Then those delights my mind might move
To live with thee, and be thy love.

Sir Walter Ralegh

THE BAIT

Come, live with me, and be my love,
And we will some new pleasures prove
Of golden sands, and crystal brooks,
With silken lines and silver hooks.

There will the river whisp'ring run,
Warm'd by thine eyes more than the Sun:
And there th' enamour'd fish will play,
Begging themselves they may betray.

When thou wilt swim in that live bath,
Each fish, which every channel hath,
Will amorously to thee swim,
Gladder to catch thee, than thou him.

If thou to be so seen art loath
By Sun or Moon, thou darken'st both;
And if myself have leave to see,
I need not their light, having thee.

Let others freeze with angling reeds,
And cut their legs with shells and weeds,
Or treacherously poor fish beset,
With strangling snare, or winding net:

Let coarse bold hands from slimy nest
The bedded fish in banks out-wrest,
Or curious traitors sleave silk flies,
Bewitch poor fishes' wand'ring eyes:

For thee, thou need'st no such deceit,
For thou thyself art thine own bait;
That fish, that is not catch'd thereby,
Alas! is wiser far than I.

John Donne

LOVE'S PHILOSOPHY

❂❂❂❂

The fountains mingle with the river,
   And the rivers with the ocean,
The winds of heaven mix forever
   With a sweet emotion;
Nothing in the world is single;
   All things by a law divine
In one another's being mingle;—
   Why not I with thine?

See the mountains kiss high heaven,
   And the waves clasp one another;
No sister flower would be forgiven
   If it disdained its brother;
And the sunlight clasps the earth,
   And the moonbeams kiss the sea;
What are all these kissings worth,
   If thou kiss not me?

Percy Bysshe Shelley

THE LADY'S "YES"

❂❂❂❂

"Yes," I answered you last night;
   "No," this morning, sir, I say.
Colors seen by candle-light
   Will not look the same by day.

When the viols played their best,
    Lamps above, and laughs below,
Love me sounded like a jest,
    Fit for *yes* or fit for *no*.

Call me false or call me free,
    Vow, whatever light may shine,
No man on your face shall see
    Any grief for change on mine.

Yet the sin is on us both;
    Time to dance is not to woo;
Wooing light makes fickle troth.
    Scorn of *me* recoils on *you*.

Learn to win a lady's faith
    Nobly, as the thing is high,
Bravely, as for life and death,
    With a loyal gravity.

Lead her from the festive boards,
    Point her to the starry skies,
Guard her, by your truthful words,
    Pure from courtship's flatteries.

By your truth she shall be true,
    Ever true, as wives of yore;
And her *yes*, once said to you,
    Shall be Yes forevermore.

Elizabeth Barrett Browning

THE COURSE
OF TRUE LOVE

from
A Midsummer Night's Dream

❖❖❖

For aught that ever I could read,
Could ever hear by tale or history,
The course of true love never did run smooth:
But, either it was different in blood,
Or else misgraffèd in respect of years;
Or else it stood upon the choice of friends;
Or, if there were a sympathy in choice,
War, death, or sickness did lay siege to it,
Making it momentary as a sound,
Swift as a shadow, short as any dream;
Brief as the lightning in the collied night,
That, in a spleen, unfolds both heaven and earth,
And ere a man hath power to say,—Behold!
The jaws of darkness do devour it up:
So quick bright things come to confusion.

William Shakespeare

THOSE EYES
❖❖❖

Ah! do not wanton with those eyes,
Lest I be sick with seeing;
Nor cast them down, but let them rise,
Lest shame destroy their being.

Ah! be not angry with those fires,
    For then their threats will kill me;
Nor look too kind on my desires,
    For then my hopes will spill me.

Ah! do not steep them in thy tears,
    For so will sorrow slay me;
Nor spread them as distraught with fears, —
    Mine own enough betray me.

Ben Jonson

SONG

ㅇ┼ㅇ┼ㅇ

My silks and fine array,
My smiles and languish'd air,
By love are driv'n away;
And mournful lean Despair
Brings me yew to deck my grave:
Such end true lovers have.

His face is fair as heav'n
When springing buds unfold
O why to him was 't giv'n
Whose heart is wintry cold?
His breast is love's all worship'd tomb,
Where all love's pilgrims come.

Bring me an axe and spade,
Bring me a winding sheet;
When I my grave have made

Let winds and tempests beat:
Then down I'll lie as cold as clay.
True love doth pass away!

William Blake

["SHALL I COME, SWEET LOVE, TO THEE"]

Shall I come, sweet love, to thee,
   When the evening beams are set?
Shall I not excluded be?
   Will you find no feigned let?
Let me not, for pity, more,
Tell the long hours at your door!

Who can tell what thief or foe,
   In the covert of the night,
For his prey will work my woe,
   Or through wicked foul despite?
So may I die unredrest,
Ere my long love be possest.

But to let such dangers pass,
   Which a lover's thoughts disdain,
'Tis enough in such a place
   To attend love's joys in vain.
Do not mock me in thy bed,
While these cold nights freeze me dead.

Thomas Campion

WHY ART THOU SILENT!

◊✦◊✦◊

Why art thou silent! Is thy love a plant
Of such weak fibre that the treacherous air
Of absence withers what was once so fair?
Is there no debt to pay, no boon to grant?
Yet have my thoughts for thee been vigilant
(As would my deeds have been) with hourly care,
The mind's least generous wish a mendicant
For nought but what thy happiness could spare.
Speak, though this soft warm heart, once free to
    hold
A thousand tender pleasures, thine and mine,
Be left more desolate, more dreary cold
Than a forsaken bird's-nest filled with snow
'Mid its own bush of leafless eglantine;
Speak, that my torturing doubts their end may
    know!

William Wordsworth

SLEEP

◊✦◊✦◊

Lock up, fair lids, the treasure of my heart;
   Preserve those beams, this age's only light;
To her sweet sense, sweet sleep some ease impart,
   Her sense, too weak to bear her spirit's might.
   And while, O sleep, thou closest up her sight,

Her sight, where Love did forge his fairest dart,
  O harbour all her parts in easeful plight;
Let no strange dream make her fair body start.
But yet, O dream if thou wilt not depart
  In this rare subject from thy common right,
  But wilt thyself in such a seat delight,
Then take my shape, and play a lover's part:
    Kiss her from me, and say unto her sprite,
    Till her eyes shine I live in darkest night.

Sir Philip Sidney

UNDER GREY SKIES

Under grey skies we stood that night,
  We two, and saw, below us there,
The city twinkling light on light.
  Behind, the long road glimmered bare
'Twixt shadowy hedges, faint and white,
  And heavy hung the silent air.

Dimly I saw the fair pale face
  Uplifted, like a slender flower
In some forgotten garden-place,
  That, at the solemn twilight hour,
Through leaves that cross and interlace,
  Craves from the night her dewy dower.

And all my heart went out to thine,
  And the lips trembled, as to show
The fire of love that might not shine;
  For, through the glamour and the glow,
I felt the clear eyes turned on mine,
  That knew not love, and could not know.

Under grey skies I stand again,
  And far beneath me, down the hill,
The gas-lamps glimmer through the rain.
  As it was then, the night is chill,
And no one knows the secret pain
  That holds the sad heart lonely still.

S. Cornish Watkins

CYNTHIA

❃❃❃❃

Away with these self-loving lads,
Whom Cupid's arrow never glads!
Away, poor souls that sigh and weep,
In love of those that lie asleep!
    For Cupid is a meadow-god,
    And forceth none to kiss the rod.

Sweet Cupid's shafts like destiny
Do causeless good or ill decree;
Desert is born out of his bow,
Reward upon his wing doth go.
    What fools are they that have not known
    That Love likes no laws but his own!

My songs they be of Cynthia's praise,
I wear her rings on holidays,
In every tree I write her name,
And every day I read the same.
Where honour Cupid's rival is,
There miracles are seen of his.

If Cynthia crave her ring of me,
I blot her name out of the tree;
If doubt do darken things held dear,
Then well-fare nothing once a year;
For many run but one must win,
Fools only hedge the cuckoo in.

The worth that worthiness should move,
Is love; that is the bow of love;
And love as well the foster can,
As can the mighty nobleman.
Sweet saint, 'tis true you worthy be,
Yet without love nought worth to me.

Fulke Greville, Lord Brooke

from *IN MEMORIAM*

C X X X

Thy voice is on the rolling air;
   I hear thee where the waters run;
   Thou standest in the rising sun,
And in the setting thou art fair.

What art thou, then? I cannot guess;
   But though I seem in star and flower
   To feel thee, some diffusive power,
I do not therefore love thee less:

My love involves the love before;
   My love is vaster passion now;
   Though mixed with God and Nature thou,
I seem to love thee more and more.

Far off thou art, but ever nigh;
   I have thee still, and I rejoice;
   I prosper, circled with thy voice;
I shall not lose thee, though I die.

Alfred, Lord Tennyson

MY TRUE-LOVE
HATH MY HEART

◊✦◊✦◊

My true-love hath my heart, and I have his,
By just exchange one for another given:
I hold his dear, and mine he cannot miss,
There never was a better bargain driven:
  My true-love hath my heart, and I have his.

His heart in me keeps him and me in one,
My heart in him his thoughts and senses guides:
He loves my heart, for once it was his own,
I cherish his because in me it bides:
  My true-love hath my heart, and I have his.

Sir Philip Sidney

SONNET XVIII

◊✦◊✦◊

Shall I compare thee to a summer's day?
Thou are more lovely and more temperate.
Rough winds do shake the darling buds of May,
And summer's lease hath all too short a date:
Sometimes too hot the eye of heaven shines,
And often is his gold complexion dimmed:
And every fair from fair sometime declines,
By chance, or nature's changing course, untrimmed:
But thy eternal summer shall not fade

Nor lose possession of that fair thou owest;
Nor shall Death brag thou wanderest in his shade
When in eternal lines to time thou growest.
So long as men can breathe or eyes can see
So long lives this, and this gives life to thee.

William Shakespeare

TO HELEN

✪✦✪✦✪

Helen, thy beauty is to me
   Like those Nicean barks of yore,
That gently, o'er a perfumed sea,
   The weary, wayworn wanderer bore
   To his own native shore.

On desperate seas long wont to roam,
   Thy hyacinth hair, thy classic face,
Thy Naiad airs have brought me home
   To the glory that was Greece,
   And the grandeur that was Rome.

Lo! in yon brilliant window-niche
   How statue-like I see thee stand,
The agate lamp within thy hand!
   Ah, Psyche, from the regions which
   Are Holy Land!

Edgar Allan Poe

TO HELEN

(After seeing her bowl
with her usual success.)

✿✿✿

Helen, thy bowling is to me
  Like that wise Alfred Shaw's of yore,
Which gently broke the wickets three:
  From Alfred few could smack a four:
    Most difficult to score!

The music of the moaning sea,
  The rattle of the flying bails,
The grey sad spires, the tawny sails—
  What memories they bring to me,
    Beholding thee!

Upon our old monastic pitch,
  How sportsmanlike I see thee stand!
The leather in thy lily hand,
  Oh, Helen of the yorkers, which
    Are nobly planned!

Andrew Lang

BELIEVE ME,
IF ALL THOSE ENDEARING
YOUNG CHARMS

❂❂❂

Believe me, if all those endearing young charms,
　　Which I gaze on so fondly to-day,
Were to change by to-morrow, and fleet in my
　　　arms,
　　Like fairy-gifts, fading away!
Thou wouldst still be ador'd, as this moment thou
　　　art,
　　Let thy loveliness fade as it will,
And, around the dear ruin, each wish of my heart
　　Would entwine itself verdantly still!

It is not, while beauty and youth are thine own,
　　And thy cheeks unprofan'd by a tear,
That the fervour and faith of a soul can be known,
　　To which time will but make thee more dear!
No, the heart that has truly lov'd, never forgets,
　　But as truly loves on to the close,
As the sun-flower turns on her god, when he sets,
　　The same look which she turn'd when he rose!

Thomas Moore

DAY AND NIGHT

All day the glorious Sun caressed
  Wide meadows and white winding way,
And on the Earth's soft heaving breast
  Heart-warm his royal kisses lay.
She looked up in his face and smiled,
  With mists of love her face seemed dim;
The golden Emperor was beguiled,
  To dream she would be true to him.

Yet was there, 'neath his golden shower,
  No end of love for him astir;
She waited, dreaming, for the hour
  When Night, her love, should come to her;
When 'neath Night's mantle she should creep
  And feel his arms about her cling,
When the soft tears true lovers weep
  Should make amends for everything.

E. Nesbit

["AND WOULD YOU SEE MY MISTRESS' FACE?"]

And would you see my mistress' face?
It is a flowery garden place,
Where knots of beauties have such grace
That all is work and nowhere space.

It is a sweet delicious morn,
Where day is breeding, never born;
It is a meadow, yet unshorn,
Which thousand flowers do adorn.

It is the heaven's bright reflex,
Weak eyes to dazzle and to vex:
It is th' Idea of her sex,
Envy of whom doth world perplex.

It is a face of Death that smiles,
Pleasing, though it kills the whiles:
Where Death and Love in pretty wiles
Each other mutually beguiles.

It is fair beauty's freshest youth,
It is the feigned Elizium's truth:
The spring, that wintered hearts reneweth:
And this is that my soul pursueth.

Thomas Campion

from THE SONG OF SOLOMON

5:9–16

❖❖❖❖

My beloved is white and ruddy, the chiefest
    among ten thousand.

His head is as the most fine gold, his locks
    are bushy, and black as a raven.

His eyes are as the eyes of doves by the
    rivers of waters, washed with milk, and
    fitly set.

His cheeks are as a bed of spices, as sweet
    flowers: his lips like lilies, dropping
    sweet smelling myrrh.

His hands are as gold rings set with the
    beryl: his belly is as bright ivory
    overlaid with sapphires.

His legs are as pillars of marble, set upon
    sockets of fine gold: his countenance is
    as Lebanon, excellent as the cedars.

His mouth is most sweet: yea, he is altogether
    lovely. This is my beloved, and this is
    my friend, O daughters of Jerusalem.

LOVE NOT ME FOR
COMELY GRACE

❂❖❂❖❂

Love not me for comely grace,
For my pleasing eye or face,
Nor for any outward part,
No, nor for my constant heart;
    For those may fail or turn to ill,
      So thou and I shall sever;
Keep therefore a true woman's eye,
And love me still, but know not why.
    So hast thou the same reason still
      To dote upon me ever.

Anonymous

SONNETS FROM THE
PORTUGUESE

XIV

❂❖❂❖❂

If thou must love me, let it be for naught
Except for love's sake only. Do not say
"I love her for her smile . . . her look . . . her way
Of speaking gently,—for a trick of thought
That falls in well with mine, and certes brought
A sense of pleasant ease on such a day."

For these things in themselves, beloved, may
Be changed, or change for thee,—and love so
    wrought,
May be unwrought so. Neither love me for
Thine own dear pity's wiping my cheeks dry,—
A creature might forget to weep, who bore
Thy comfort long, and lose thy love thereby.
But love me for love's sake, that evermore
Thou mayst love on, through love's eternity.

Elizabeth Barrett Browning

HE THAT LOVES A
ROSY CHEEK

❁❁❁❁

He that loves a rosy cheek,
    Or a coral lip admires,
Or from starlike eyes doth seek
    Fuel to maintain his fires;
As old Time makes these decay,
So his flames must waste away.

But a smooth and steadfast mind
    Gentle thoughts, and calm desires,
Hearts with equal love combined,
    Kindle never-dying fires:—
Where these are not, I despise
Lovely cheeks or lips or eyes.

Thomas Carew

SONNETS FROM THE PORTUGUESE

XLII

❂❂❂

How do I love thee? Let me count the ways.
I love thee to the depth and breadth and height
My soul can reach, when feeling out of sight
For the ends of Being and ideal Grace.
I love thee to the level of every day's
Most quiet need, by sun and candle-light.
I love thee freely, as men strive for right;
I love thee purely, as they turn from praise.
I love thee with the passion put to use
In my old griefs, and with my childhood's faith.
I love thee with a love I seemed to lose
With my lost saints—I love thee with the breath,
Smiles, tears, of all my life!—and, if God choose,
I shall but love thee better after death.

Elizabeth Barrett Browning

SHE WALKS IN BEAUTY

She walks in beauty, like the night
   Of cloudless climes and starry skies,
And all that's best of dark and bright
   Meets in her aspect and her eyes,
Thus mellowed to that tender light
   Which heaven to gaudy day denies.

One shade the more, one ray the less
   Had half impaired the nameless grace
Which waves in every raven tress
   Or softly lightens o'er her face,
Where thoughts serenely sweet express
   How pure, how dear their dwelling-place.

And on that cheek and o'er that brow
   So soft, so calm, yet eloquent,
The smiles that win, the tints that glow,
   But tell of days in goodness spent,—
A mind at peace with all below,
   A heart whose love is innocent.

George Gordon, Lord Byron

WHENAS IN SILKS MY JULIA GOES

❂❀❂❀❂

Whenas in silks my Julia goes
Then, then (methinks) how sweetly flows
That liquefaction of her clothes.

Next, when I cast mine eyes and see
That brave vibration each way free;
O, how that glittering taketh me!

Robert Herrick

OUT OF THE ROLLING OCEAN THE CROWD

Out of the rolling ocean the crowd came a drop
      gently to me,
Whispering, I love you, before long I die,
I have travel'd a long way merely to look on you to
      touch you,
For I could not die till I once look'd on you,
For fear'd I might afterward lose you.

Now we have met, we have look'd, we are safe,
Return in peace to the ocean my love,
I too am part of that ocean my love, we are not so
      much separated,
Behold the great rondure, the cohesion of all, how
      perfect!
But as for me, for you, the irresistible sea is to
      separate us,
As for an hour carrying us diverse, yet cannot carry
      us diverse forever;
Be not impatient—a little space—know you I salute
      the air, the ocean and the land,
Every day at sundown for your dear sake my love.

Walt Whitman

EROS

The sense of the world is short, —
Long and various the report, —
    To love and be beloved;
Men and gods have not outlearned it;
And, how oft soe'er they've turned it,
    Not to be improved.

Ralph Waldo Emerson

INVOCATION TO THE ANGEL

from *Heaven and Earth*

Samiasa!
I call thee, I await thee, and I love thee;
    Many may worship thee, that will I not;
If that thy spirit down to mine may move thee,
    Descend and share my lot!
      Though I be formed of clay,
        And thou of beams
      More bright than those of day
        On Eden's streams,

Thine immortality cannot repay
    With love more warm than mine
My love. There is a ray
    In me, which, though forbidden yet to shine,
    I feel was lighted at thy God's and thine.
It may be hidden long: death and decay
    Our mother Eve bequeathed us, but my heart
Defies it; though this life must pass away,
    Is *that* a cause for thee and me to part?
Thou art immortal; so am I: I feel—
    I feel my immortality o'ersweep
All pains, all tears, all time, all fears, and peal,
    Like the eternal thunders of the deep,
Into my ears this truth,— "Thou liv'st forever!"

                              George Gordon, Lord Byron

STRANGE FITS OF
PASSION
HAVE I KNOWN

ᴏᴛᴏᴛᴏ

Strange fits of passion have I known:
And I will dare to tell,
But in the Lover's ear alone,
What once to me befel.

When she I loved was strong and gay,
And like a rose in June,
I to her cottage bent my way,
Beneath the evening moon.

Upon the moon I fixed my eye,
All over the wide lea;
My horse trudged on—and we drew nigh
Those paths so dear to me.

And now we reached the orchard plot;
And, as we climbed the hill,
Towards the roof of Lucy's cot
The moon descended still.

In one of those sweet dreams I slept,
Kind Nature's gentlest boon!
And all the while my eyes I kept
On the descending moon.

My horse moved on; hoof after hoof
He raised, and never stopped;
When down behind the cottage roof,
At once, the bright moon dropped.

What fond and wayward thoughts will slide
Into a lover's head!—
"O mercy!" to myself I cried,
"If Lucy should be dead!"

William Wordsworth

SONNET

from *Amoretti*

What guile is this, that those her golden tresses,
   She doth attire under a net of gold;
And with sly skill so cunningly them dresses,
   That which is gold or hair, may scarce be told?
   Is it that men's frail eyes, which gaze too bold,
She may entangle in that golden snare:
   And being caught may craftily enfold,
Their weaker hearts, which are not well aware?
Take heed therefore, mine eyes, how ye do stare
   Henceforth too rashly on that guileful net,
In which if ever ye entrapped are,
   Out of her bands ye by no means shall get.
      Fondness it were for any being free,
      To covet fetters, though they golden be.

Edmund Spenser

KISSING HER HAIR

✧✦✧✦✧

Kissing her hair, I sat against her feet:
Wove and unwove it,—wound, and found it sweet;
Made fast therewith her hands, drew down her eyes,
Deep as deep flowers, and dreamy like dim skies;
With her own tresses bound, and found her fair,—
    Kissing her hair.

Sleep were no sweeter than her face to me,—
Sleep of cold sea-bloom under the cold sea:
What pain could get between my face and hers?
What new sweet thing would Love not relish worse?
Unless, perhaps, white Death had kissed me there,—
    Kissing her hair.

Algernon Charles Swinburne

I DO NOT LOVE THEE
FOR THAT FAIR

✧✦✧✦✧

I do not love thee for that fair
Rich fan of thy most curious hair,
Though the wires thereof be drawn
Finer than the threads of lawn,
And are softer than the leaves
On which the subtle spider weaves.

I do not love thee for those flowers
Growing on thy cheeks,—love's bowers,—
Though such cunning them hath spread,
None can paint them white and red.
Love's golden arrows thence are shot,
Yet for them I love thee not.

I do not love thee for those soft
Red coral lips I've kissed so oft;
Nor teeth of pearl, the double guard
To speech whence music still is heard,
Though from those lips a kiss being taken
Might tyrants melt, and death awaken.

I do not love thee, O my fairest,
For that richest, for that rarest
Silver pillar, which stands under
Thy sound head, that globe of wonder;
Though that neck be whiter far
Than towers of polished ivory are.

Thomas Carew

IN PATHS UNTRODDEN

In paths untrodden,
In the growth by margins of pond-waters,
Escaped from the life that exhibits itself,
From all the standards hitherto publish'd,
    from the pleasures, profits, conformities,
Which too long I was offering to feed my soul,
Clear to me now standards not yet publish'd, clear
    to me that my soul,
That the soul of the man I speak for rejoices in
    comrades,
Here by myself away from the clank of the world,
Tallying and talk'd to here by tongues aromatic,
No longer abash'd, (for in this secluded spot I
    can respond as I would not dare elsewhere,)
Strong upon me the life that does not exhibit itself,
    yet contains all the rest,
Resolv'd to sing no songs to-day but those of manly
    attachment,
Projecting them along that substantial life,
Bequeathing hence types of athletic love,
Afternoon this delicious Ninth-month in my forty-
    first year,
I proceed for all who are or have been young men,

To tell the secret of my nights and days,
To celebrate the need of comrades.

Walt Whitman

SONNET

from *Amoretti*

✿✿✿✿

Oft when my spirit doth spread her bolder wings,
   In mind to mount up to the purest sky,
It down is weighed with thought of earthly things
   And clogged with burden of mortality,
   Where when that sovereign beauty it doth spy,
Resembling heaven's glory in her light,
   Drawn with sweet pleasure's bait, it back doth fly,
And unto heaven forgets her former flight.
There my frail fancy, fed with full delight,
   Doth bathe in bliss and mantleth most at ease:
Ne thinks of other heaven, but how it might
   Her heart's desire with most contentment please.
     Heart need not with none other happiness,
     But here on earth to have such heaven's bliss.

Edmund Spenser

PHILLIDA AND CORIDON

A PASTORAL

In the merry month of May,
In a morn by break of day,
Forth I walked by the wood side,
When as May was in his pride,
There I spied all alone
Phillida and Coridon.
Much ado there was; God wot
He would love and she would not;
She said, never man was true;
He said, none was false to you.
He said, he had lov'd her long;
She said, love should have no wrong.
Coridon would kiss her then;
She said, maids must kiss no men
Till they did for good and all:
Then she made the shepherd call
All the heavens to witness truth;
Never lov'd a truer youth.
Then with many a pretty oath,
Yea and nay, and faith and troth;
Such as silly shepherds use,
When they will not love abuse;
Love, which had been long deluded,
Was with kisses sweet concluded;
And Phillida with garlands gay
Was made the Lady of the May.

Nicholas Breton

LA BELLE DAME
SANS MERCI

"O what can ail thee, knight-at-arms,
  Alone and palely loitering?
The sedge is wither'd from the lake,
  And no birds sing.

"O what can ail thee, knight-at-arms,
  So haggard and so woe-begone?
The squirrel's granary is full,
  And the harvest's done.

"I see a lily on thy brow
  With anguish moist and fever dew;
And on thy cheek a fading rose
  Fast withereth too."

"I met a lady in the meads,
  Full beautiful—a faery's child,
Her hair was long, her foot was light,
  And her eyes were wild.

"I made a garland for her head,
  And bracelets too, and fragrant zone;
She look'd at me as she did love,
  And made sweet moan.

"I set her on my pacing steed
  And nothing else saw all day long,
For sideways would she lean, and sing
  A faery's song.

"She found me roots of relish sweet,
   And honey wild and manna dew,
And sure in language strange she said,
     'I love thee true!'

"She took me to her elfin grot,
   And there she wept and sigh'd full sore;
And there I shut her wild, wild eyes
     With kisses four.

"And there she lullèd me asleep,
   And there I dream'd—Ah! woe betide!
The latest dream I ever dream'd
     On the cold hill's side.

"I saw pale kings and princes too,
   Pale warriors, death-pale were they all;
Who cried—'La belle Dame sans Merci
     Hath thee in thrall!'

"I saw their starved lips in the gloam
   With horrid warning gapèd wide,
And I awoke and found me here
     On the cold hill's side.

"And this is why I sojourn here
   Alone and palely loitering,
Though the sedge is wither'd from the lake,
     And no birds sing."

John Keats

A RED, RED ROSE

O my Luve's like a red, red rose
   That's newly sprung in June:
O my Luve's like the melodie
   That's sweetly played in tune.
As fair art thou, my bonnie lass,
   So deep in luve am I:
And I will luve thee still, my dear,
   Till a' the seas gang dry:

Till a' the seas gang dry, my dear,
   And the rocks melt wi' the sun;
I will luve thee still, my dear,
   While the sands o' life shall run.
And fare thee weel, my only Luve!
   And fare thee weel awhile!
And I will come again, my Luve,
   Tho' it were ten thousand mile.

Robert Burns

MEETING AT NIGHT

❁❁❁

The gray sea and the long black land;
And the yellow half-moon large and low;
And the startled little waves that leap
In fiery ringlets from their sleep,
As I gain the cove with pushing prow,
And quench its speed i' the slushy sand.

Then a mile of warm sea-scented beach;
Three fields to cross till a farm appears;
A tap at the pane, the quick sharp scratch
And blue spurt of a lighted match,
And a voice less loud, through its joys and fears,
Than the two hearts beating each to each!

Robert Browning

PARTING AT MORNING

❁❁❁

Round the cape of a sudden came the sea,
And the sun looked over the mountain's rim:
And straight was a path of gold for him,
And the need of a world of men for me.

Robert Browning

ALAS! HOW LIGHT A CAUSE MAY MOVE—

from *The Light of the Harem*

✧✦✧✦✧

Alas! how light a cause may move
Dissension between hearts that love!—
Hearts that the world in vain has tried,
And sorrow but more closely tied;
That stood the storm when waves were rough,
Yet in a sunny hour fall off,
Like ships that have gone down at sea,
When heaven was all tranquillity!
A something light as air,—a look,
  A word unkind or wrongly taken,—
O, love that tempests never shook,
  A breath, a touch like this has shaken!
And ruder words will soon rush in
To spread the breach that words begin;
And eyes forget the gentle ray
They wore in courtship's smiling day;
And voices lose the tone that shed
A tenderness round all they said;
Till fast declining, one by one,
The sweetnesses of love are gone,
And hearts, so lately mingled, seem
Like broken clouds,—or like the stream,
That smiling left the mountain's brow,
  As though its waters ne'er could sever,
Yet, ere it reach the plain below,
  Breaks into floods that part forever.

O you, that have the charge of Love,
    Keep him in rose bondage bound,
As in the Fields of Bliss above
    He sits, with flowerets fettered round;—
Loose not a tie that round him clings,
Nor ever let him use his wings;
For even an hour, a minute's flight
Will rob the plumes of half their light.
Like that celestial bird,—whose nest
    Is found beneath far Eastern skies,—
Whose wings, though radiant when at rest,
    Lose all their glory when he flies!

Thomas Moore

FAREWELL

Farewell! if ever fondest prayer
    For other's weal availed on high,
Mine will not all be lost in air,
    But waft thy name beyond the sky.
'Twere vain to speak, to weep, to sigh:
    Oh! more than tears of blood can tell,
When wrung from guilt's expiring eye,
    Are in that word—Farewell!—Farewell!

These lips are mute, these eyes are dry;
    But in my breast and in my brain,
Awake the pangs that pass not by,
    The thought that ne'er shall sleep again.

My soul nor deigns nor dares complain,
  Though grief and passion there rebel:
I only know we loved in vain;
  I only feel—Farewell!—Farewell!

George Gordon, Lord Byron

AN EARNEST SUIT

To his unkind mistress
not to forsake him

❁❀❁

And wilt thou leave me thus?
Say nay! say nay! for shame!
To save thee from the blame
Of all my grief and grame.
And wilt thou leave me thus?
  Say nay! say nay!

And wilt thou leave me thus,
That hath loved thee so long,
In wealth and woe among?
And is thy heart so strong
As for to leave me thus?
  Say nay! say nay!

And wilt thou leave me thus,
That hath given thee my heart,
Never for to depart,

Neither for pain nor smart?
And wilt thou leave me thus?
    Say nay! say nay!

And wilt thou leave me thus,
And have no more pity
Of him that loveth thee?
Alas! thy cruelty!
And wilt thou leave me thus?
    Say nay! say nay!

Sir Thomas Wyatt

"THE CLOSED MANUSCRIPT"

✿✦✿✦✿

"Alas! that youth's sweet scented manuscript should
  close."
                —*Rubaiyat of Omar Khayyam*

I

In youth's sweet scented manuscript we wrote,
All through the perfect, rosy summer days,
And when the nightingale's delicious note
Toned with love's orison, in reverent praise
We chronicled our joy with pencilled lays—
In that sweet scented manuscript we wrote.

II

All night embalmed in rose leaves soft 'twas laid,
Till the pale parchment glowed with rose tints rare,
As fainting lips from which the blood has strayed
Glow when requickened; and the perfume there
Tinged with its subtle essence all the air—
Since all night long embalmed so soft 'twas laid.

III

Alas! we rolled it up one cloudy day,
When the rude winds of autumn ruffled it.
Torn was the leaf whereon no writing lay,
Yellow, it seemed, by no rose radiance lit.
And never more we twain therein have writ
Since it was folded up that cloudy day!

IV

Bury it somewhere, Love, for ever rolled,
(Perchance some leaves shall always sweet remain)
Beneath a rose-tree, in the soft, dark mould,
For this same summer shall not come again.
Oh! lest we mar it with our tears, our pain—
Bury it somewhere, Love, for ever rolled!

Constance Finch

["WHEN THE LAMP IS SHATTERED"]

When the lamp is shattered
The light in the dust lies dead;
When the cloud is scattered,
The rainbow's glory is shed.
When the lute is broken,
Sweet tones are remembered not;
When the lips have spoken,
Loved accents are soon forgot.

As music and splendor
Survive not the lamp and the lute,
The heart's echoes render
No song when the spirit is mute,—
No song but sad dirges,
Like the wind through a ruined cell,
Or the mournful surges
That ring the dead seaman's knell.

When hearts have once mingled,
Love first leaves the well-built nest;
The weak one is singled
To endure what it once possesst.
O Love! who bewailest
The frailty of all things here,
Why choose you the frailest
For your cradle, your home, and your bier?

Its passions will rock thee
As the storms rock the ravens on high;

Bright reason will mock thee
Like the sun from a wintry sky.
From thy nest every rafter
Will rot, and thine eagle home
Leave thee naked to laughter,
When leaves fall and cold winds come.

Percy Bysshe Shelley

WE'LL GO
NO MORE A-ROVING

So, we'll go no more a-roving
　　So late into the night,
Though the heart be still as loving,
　　And the moon be still as bright.

For the sword outwears its sheath,
　　And the soul wears out the breast,
And the heart must pause to breathe,
　　And love itself have rest.

Though the night was made for loving,
　　And the day returns too soon,
Yet we'll go no more a-roving
　　By the light of the moon.

George Gordon, Lord Byron

SWEET AND LOW

Sweet and low, sweet and low,
    Wind of the western sea,
Low, low, breathe and blow,
    Wind of the western sea!
Over the rolling waters go,
Come from the dying moon, and blow,
    Blow him again to me;
While my little one, while my pretty one, sleeps.

Sleep and rest, sleep and rest,
    Father will come to thee soon;
Rest, rest, on mother's breast,
    Father will come to thee soon;
Father will come to his babe in the nest,
Silver sails all out of the west
    Under the silver moon:
Sleep, my little one, sleep, my pretty one, sleep.

Alfred, Lord Tennyson

TO ELLEN

And Ellen, when the graybeard years
    Have brought us to life's evening hour,
And all the crowded Past appears
    A tiny scene of sun and shower,

Then, if I read the page aright
    Where Hope, the soothsayer, reads our lot,
Thyself shalt own the page was bright,
    Well that we loved, woe had we not,

When Mirth is dumb and Flattery's fled,
    And mute thy music's dearest tone,
When all but Love itself is dead
    And all but deathless Reason gone.

                        Ralph Waldo Emerson

THE AGE OF WISDOM

Ho! pretty page, with the dimpled chin,
    That never has known the barber's shear,
All your wish is woman to win;

This is the way that boys begin,—
    Wait till you come to forty year.

Curly gold locks cover foolish brains;
    Billing and cooing is all your cheer,—
Sighing, and singing of midnight strains,
Under Bonnybell's window-panes,—
    Wait till you come to forty year.

Forty times over let Michaelmas pass;
    Grizzling hair the brain doth clear;
Then you know a boy is an ass,
Then you know the worth of a lass,—
    Once you have come to forty year.

Pledge me round; I bid ye declare,
    All good fellows whose beards are gray,—
Did not the fairest of the fair
Common grow and wearisome ere
    Ever a month was past away?

The reddest lips that ever have kissed,
    The brightest eyes that ever have shone,
May pray and whisper and we not list,
Or look away and never be missed,—
    Ere yet ever a month is gone.

Gillian's dead! God rest her bier,—
    How I loved her twenty years syne!
Marian's married; but I sit here,
Alone and merry at forty year,
    Dipping my nose in the Gascon wine.

                              William Makepeace Thackeray

SHE WAS A PHANTOM
OF DELIGHT

She was a phantom of delight
When first she gleamed upon my sight;
A lovely apparition, sent
To be a moment's ornament;
Her eyes as stars of twilight fair;
Like Twilight's, too, her dusky hair;
But all things else about her drawn
From May-time and the cheerful dawn;
A dancing shape, an image gay,
To haunt, to startle, and waylay.

I saw her upon nearer view,
A spirit, yet a woman too!
Her household motions light and free,
And steps of virgin-liberty;
A countenance in which did meet
Sweet records, promises as sweet;
A creature not too bright or good
For human nature's daily food,
For transient sorrows, simple wiles,
Praise, blame, love, kisses, tears, and smiles.

And now I see with eye serene
The very pulse of the machine;
A being breathing thoughtful breath,
A traveller between life and death;
The reason firm, the temperate will,
Endurance, foresight, strength, and skill;
A perfect woman, nobly planned
To warn, to comfort, and command;

And yet a spirit still, and bright
With something of an angel-light.

NEVER THE TIME AND THE PLACE
❂❂❂

Never the time and the place
   And the loved one all together!
This path—how soft to pace!
   This May—what magic weather!
Where is the loved one's face?
In a dream that loved one's face meets mine,
   But the house is narrow, the place is bleak
Where, outside, rain and wind combine
   With a furtive ear, if I strive to speak,
   With a hostile eye at my flushing cheek,
With a malice that marks each word, each sign!
O enemy sly and serpentine,
   Uncoil thee from the waking man!
     Do I hold the Past
     Thus firm and fast
   Yet doubt if the Future hold I can?
This path so soft to pace shall lead
Through the magic of May to herself indeed!
Or narrow if needs the house must be,
Outside are the storms and strangers: we—
Oh, close, safe, warm sleep I and she,—I and she!

Robert Browning

TO MY DEAR AND LOVING HUSBAND

If ever two were one, then surely we;
If ever man were loved by wife, then thee;
If ever wife was happy in a man,
Compare with me, ye women, if you can.
I prize thy love more than whole mines of gold,
Or all the riches that the East doth hold.
My love is such that rivers cannot quench,
Nor aught but love from thee give recompense.
Thy love is such I can no way repay;
The heavens reward thee manifold, I pray.
Then while we live in love let's so persevere
That when we live no more we may live ever.

Anne Bradstreet

ECHO

Come to me in the silence of the night;
  Come in the speaking silence of a dream;
Come with soft rounded cheeks and eyes as bright
  As sunlight on a stream;
    Come back in tears,
O memory, hope, love of finished years.

Oh dream how sweet, too sweet, too bitter sweet,
  Whose wakening should have been in Paradise,
Where souls brimfull of love abide and meet;
  Where thirsting longing eyes
    Watch the slow door
That opening, letting in, lets out no more.

Yet come to me in dreams, that I may live
  My very life again though cold in death:
Come back to me in dreams, that I may give
  Pulse for pulse, breath for breath:
    Speak low, lean low,
As long ago, my love, how long ago!

Christina Rossetti

ADDRESS OF RUTH
TO NAOMI

Entreat me not to leave thee,
Or to return from following after thee:
For whither thou goest,
I will go;
And where thou lodgest,
I will lodge.
Thy people shall be my people,
And thy God my God.
Where thou diest, will I die,
And there will I be buried.

The Lord do so to me, and more also,
If ought but death part thee and me.

The Book of Ruth

["I ARISE FROM DREAMS
OF THEE"]

I arise from dreams of thee
    In the first sweet sleep of night,
When the winds are breathing low,
    And the stars are shining bright.
I arise from dreams of thee,
    And a spirit in my feet
Has led me—who knows how?—
    To thy chamber-window, sweet!

The wandering airs they faint
  On the dark, the silent stream,—
The champak odors fail
  Like sweet thoughts in a dream;
The nightingale's complaint,
  It dies upon her heart,
As I must die on thine,
  O, beloved as thou art!

O, lift me from the grass!
  I die, I faint, I fail!
Let thy love in kisses rain
  On my lips and eyelids pale.
My cheek is cold and white, alas!
  My heart beats loud and fast:
Oh! press it close to thine again,
  Where it will break at last!

Percy Bysshe Shelley

BEFORE THE DAWN

In the weird stillness just before the dawn
  Low sang the waves, like murmuring tones that
    bless,
  Along the far, dim shore, by cape and ness,
And furtive winds blew soft across the lawn,
  Touching with spirit-lips in faint caress
  The virgin-lilies, white and motionless,
In the weird stillness just before the dawn.

Was it a dream, or did you really come
　'Twixt the wan glimmer of my casement, where
　The sweet wind followed you? Did I not hear
Your low voice, passion-thrilled, I, speechless,
　　dumb?
　While in the tender gloom, near and more near,
　Your fond lips drew to mine and rested there—
Was it a rapturous dream, or did you come?

Frances Nicholson

A FRAGMENT

And then it seem'd I was a bird
　That dipt along the silent street.
In that strange midnight nothing stir'd,
　And all was moonlight, still and sweet.

By lofty vane and roof and loft,
　Aloof, aloft, where shadows hung,
Down ghostly ways that wafted soft,
　Warm echoes where I sank and sung;

And lower yet by flower-set sill,
　And close against her window-bars,
And still the moonlight flowed, and still,
　The still dew lit the jessamine stars;

And oh! I beat against the pane,
　And oh! I sang so sweet, so clear,—

I heard her wake, and pause again,
　　Then nearer, nearer—killing near;

And back she flung the window-rod,
　　The moonlight swept in, like a stream;
She drew me to her neck—Oh! God,
　　'Twas then I knew it was a dream!

Theo Marzials

THE DREAM
✿✿✿✿

Dear love, for nothing less than thee
Would I have broke this happy dream,
　　　It was a theme
For reason, much too strong for fantasy.
Therefore thou wak'dst me wisely; yet
My dream thou brok'st not, but continued'st it:
Thou art so true, that thoughts of thee suffice
To make dreams truth, and fables histories;
Enter these arms, for since thou thought'st it best
Not to dream all my dream, let's act the rest.

As lightning or a taper's light,
Thine eyes, and not thy noise, wak'd me;
　　　Yet I thought thee
(For thou lov'st truth) an angel at first sight,
But when I saw thou saw'st my heart,
And knew'st my thoughts beyond an angel's art,
When thou knew'st what I dreamt, then thou
　　　knew'st when

Excess of joy would wake me, and cam'st then;
I must confess, it could not choose but be
Profane to think thee any thing but thee.

Coming and staying show'd thee thee,
But rising makes me doubt, that now
            Thou art not thou.
That love is weak, where fear 's as strong as he;
'T is not all spirit, pure and brave,
If mixture it of fear, shame, honour, have,
Perchance as torches, which must ready be,
Men light and put out, so thou deal'st with me,
Thou cam'st to kindle, goest to come: then I
Will dream that hope again, but else would die.

                                        John Donne

LONGING
❂❥❂❥❂

Come to me in my dreams, and then
By day I shall be well again!
For so the night will more than pay
The hopeless longing of the day.

Come, as thou cam'st a thousand times,
A messenger from radiant climes,
And smile on thy new world, and be
As kind to others as to me!

Or, as thou never cam'st in sooth,
Come now, and let me dream it truth;
And part my hair, and kiss my brow,
And say: *My love! why sufferest thou?*

Come to me in my dreams, and then
By day I shall be well again!
For so the night will more than pay
The hopeless longing of the day.

Matthew Arnold

from "THE NOON OF LOVE"
✧✦✧✦✧

Westward each nightfall
When white lies the dew,
Where the stream makes a bright fall
Of moon-rays for you;
While the night wind goes sighing
Over crag, over hollow,
Like a ghostly replying
To the snowy owl's crying,
I the white waters follow;
With lips still sweet from sweet lips kist,
Like a spirit I pass
O'er the gleaming grass
Into the moon and the mist.

J. A. Blaikie

I SAW TWO CLOUDS
AT MORNING

ᛩᛩᛩᛩ

I saw two clouds at morning,
    Tinged by the rising sun,
And in the dawn they floated on,
    And mingled into one;
I thought that morning cloud was blessed,
It moved so sweetly to the west.

I saw two summer currents
    Flow smoothly to their meeting,
And join their course, with silent force,
    In peace each other greeting;
Calm was their course through banks of green,
While dimpling eddies played between.

Such be your gentle motion,
    Till life's last pulse shall beat;
Like summer's beam, and summer's stream,
    Float on, in joy, to meet
A calmer sea, where storms shall cease,
A purer sky, where all is peace.

John G. C. Brainard

THE GOLDEN TOUCH

The amber dust of sunset fills
The limits of my narrow room,
And every sterile shadow thrills
To golden hope, to golden bloom.

Sweet through the splendour, shrill and sweet,
Somewhere a neighbouring cage-bird sings,
Sings of the Spring in this grey street
While golden glories gild his wings.

Clothed with the sun he breaks to song—
In vague remembrance, deep delight—
Of dim green worlds, forsaken long,
Of leaf-hung dawn and dewy night.

My prisoning bars, transfigured too,
Fade with the day, forsworn, forgot—
Melt in a golden mist—and you
Are here, although you know it not.

Rosamund Marriott Watson

from *EPITHALAMION*

Ah! when will this long weary day have end,
And lend me leave to come unto my love?
How slowly do the hours their numbers spend!

How slowly does sad Time his feathers move!
Haste thee, O fairest planet, to thy home
Within the western foam;
Thy tired steeds long since have need of rest.
Long though it be, at last I see it gloom,
And the bright evening star with golden crest
Appear out of the east.
Fair child of beauty, glorious lamp of love
That all the host of heaven in ranks dost lead,
And guidest lovers through the night's sad dread,
How cheerfully thou lookest from above,
And seem'st to laugh atween thy twinkling light,
As joying in the sight
Of these glad many which for joy do sing,
That all the woods them answer and their echo
      ring.

Edmund Spenser

["IF YOU WERE COMING IN THE FALL"]

❁❁❁❁

If you were coming in the fall,
I'd brush the summer by
With half a smile and half a spurn,
As housewives do a fly.

If I could see you in a year,
I'd wind the months in balls,
And put them each in separate drawers,
Until their time befalls.

If only centuries delayed,
I'd count them on my hand,
Subtracting till my fingers dropped
Into Van Diemen's land.

If certain, when this life was out,
That yours and mine should be,
I'd toss it yonder like a rind,
And taste eternity.

But now, all ignorant of the length
Of time's uncertain wing,
It goads me, like the goblin bee,
That will not state its sting.

Emily Dickinson

from "LOVE'S
CONSOLATION"

❀❀❀❀

All who have loved, be sure of this from me,
That to have touched one little ripple free
Of golden hair, or held a little hand
Very long since, is better than to stand
Rolled up in vestures stiff with golden thread,
Upon a throne o'er many a bowing head
Of adulators; yea, and to have seen
Thy lady walking in a garden green,
'Mid apple blossoms and green twisted boughs,

Along the golden gravel path, to house
Herself, where thou art watching far below,
Deep in thy bower impervious, even though
Thou never give her kisses after that,
Is sweeter than to never break the flat
Of thy soul's rising, like a river tide
That never foams; yea, if thy lady chide
Cruelly thy service, and indeed becomes
A wretch, whose false eyes haunt thee in all rooms,
'Tis better so, than never to have been
An hour in love; than never to have seen
Thine own heart's worthiness to shrink and shake,
Like silver quick, all for thy lady's sake,
Weighty with truth, with gentleness as bright.
    Moreover, let sad lovers take delight
In this, that time will bring at last their peace;
We watch great passions in their huge increase,
Until they fill our hearts, so that we say,
"Let go this, and I die"; yet nay and nay,
We find them leave us strangely quiet then,
When they must quit; one lion leaves the den,
Another enters; wherefore thus I cross
All lovers pale and starving with their loss.

Richard Watson Dixon

94

from "OUT OF THE CRADLE ENDLESSLY ROCKING"

Two together!
Winds blow south, or winds blow north,
Day come white, or night come black,
Home, or rivers and mountains from home,
Singing all time, minding no time,
While we two keep together.

Walt Whitman